EARTH
ELEMENTAL EARTH

BY
WILLIAM ANTHONY

Cavendish Square

New York

Published in 2021 by Cavendish Square Publishing, LLC
243 5th Avenue, Suite 136, New York, NY 10016

Copyright © 2021 Booklife Publishing
This edition published by agreement with Booklife Publishing

First Edition

Website: cavendishsq.com

This publication represents the opinions and views of the author based on his or her personal experience, knowledge,
and research. The information in this book serves as a general guide only. The author and publisher have used their best
efforts in preparing this book and disclaim liability rising directly or indirectly from the use and application of this book.
All websites were available and accurate when this book was sent to press.

Cataloging-in-Publication Data

Names: Anthony, William.
Title: Earth / William Anthony.
Description: New York : Cavendish Square, 2021. | Series: Elemental Earth | Includes glossary and index.
Identifiers: ISBN 9781502657930 (pbk.) | ISBN 9781502657954 (library bound) |
ISBN 9781502657947 (6 pack) | ISBN 9781502657961 (ebook)
Subjects: LCSH: Geology--Juvenile literature. | Four elements (Philosophy)--Juvenile literature. | Earth (Planet)--Juvenile literature.
Classification: LCC QE29 A584 2021 | DDC 551--dc23

Written by: William Anthony
Edited by: Kirsty Holmes
Designed by: Drue Rintoul

Printed in the United States of America

CPSIA compliance information: Batch #CS20CSQ.
For further information contact Cavendish Square Publishing LLC, New York, New York, at 1-877-980-4450.

CONTENTS

Words that look like **THIS** are explained in the glossary on page 31.

BATTLE OF THE ELEMENTS

Earth is in exacty the right place in our solar system to support life. It has air with **OXYGEN** and **CARBON DIOXIDE** to allow animals to breathe and plants to **PHOTOSYNTHESIZE**. It has a lot of water for animals and plants to use. It has materials for making fire naturally, and it has soil that helps plants, animals, and people live and grow.

DESTRUCTION!

Earth, air, water, and fire are central to everything on our planet, and we call them the four elements. Although these elements of Earth can be helpful, they can also be destructive. Water, fire, earth, and air are all able to support life on our planet, but they can also take lives away. Floods can destroy homes, fires can burn down huge areas of land, winds can damage buildings, and earthquakes can make bridges collapse.

Natural disasters occur when the natural elements cause destruction. Examples include hurricanes and earthquakes.

damage from Indonesian earthquake

ELEMENTS IN GREECE

The ancient Greeks believed everything on Earth was made from at least one of four elements. This way of thinking shaped science, medicine, and *PHILOSOPHY* for the next 2,000 years. Modern science has taught us that this theory isn't entirely true, but the ancient Greeks weren't too far off either. We now understand that all *MATTER* is either a solid (like earth), a liquid (like water), a gas (like air), or a *PLASMA* (like some kinds of fire).

The ancient Greeks were one of the first *CIVILIZATIONS* in history to develop a system of mathematics.

POWERFUL TOOLS

We now know enough about the four elements to harness their power in unique ways. We can use them to make electricity to power our cities. We can use them to help us travel from place to place. We can even use them to help build our homes. The elements can be dangerous, but they can also be very helpful for humans.

Some houses are made from mud bricks.

5

THE WORLD'S LARGEST JIGSAW PUZZLE

From a distance, it might seem that our planet is nothing but large areas of land and huge oceans of water; look closer and you will see beyond the surface. Underneath the land and water, there is a lot more going on than might meet the eye: it's the world's largest jigsaw puzzle—the Earth's **CRUST**!

This surface layer of our planet is between 18 and 31 miles (30 and 50 km) thick under the **CONTINENTS**, and around 3 to 6 miles (5 to 10 km) thick under the oceans. This might sound like a lot, but it is only 1% of Earth's **VOLUME**.

The Earth's crust is the outermost layer of our planet.

PUZZLE PIECES

The vast majority of Earth's crust is made from seven large puzzle pieces called tectonic plates. They sit above the Earth's **MANTLE**, which is constantly moving and causes the plates to shift slightly over time. Tectonic plates can move toward each other, away from each other, or grind along each other by moving side to side.

Tectonic plates move between 0.75 and 2 inches (2 and 5 centimeters) every year, which is about the same rate as your fingernails grow!

NORTH AMERICAN PLATE

Juan de Fuca plate

EURASIAN PLATE

AMERICA PLATE

Arabian plate

Indian plate

Caribbean plate

Cocos plate

AFRICAN PLATE

Philippine Plate

PACIFIC PLATE

PACIFIC PLATE

Nazca plate

SOUTH AMERICAN PLATE

AUSTRALIAN PLATE

These are the tectonic plates.

Scotia Plate

ANTARCTIC PLATE

EURASIA

NORTH
AMERICA

AFRICA

SOUTH
AMERICA

INDIA

ANTARCTICA
AUSTRALIA

This map of
Pangaea shows
where some of the
continents and countries we know today have come from.

A VERY DIFFERENT WORLD

Although the tectonic plates might not seem to move that much in a single year, over millions of years it adds up to a lot! Some of Earth's tectonic plates have moved thousands of miles over their lifetimes. Around 250 million years ago, all of Earth's continents were bound together as one huge supercontinent called Pangaea. Between then and now, the tectonic plates have moved thousands of miles and broken Pangaea apart to form the world we know today.

GIVE AND TAKE

Movements in Earth's crust can transform or destroy parts of our planet. As the tectonic plates come toward each other, huge mountain ranges and volcanoes are created. As the plates move away from each other, huge *FAULTS* are created. Even a couple of centimeters of movement from side to side can cause devastating earthquakes. We can create homes from the earth—but it can easily destroy them as well.

Movements in the plates can cause up to 14,000 earthquakes and 80 volcanic eruptions every year.

ON SHAKY GROUND

EARTHQUAKES

Natural disasters are common occurrences when it comes to our planet's four elements, and earth is no different. When the ground rumbles underneath your feet, this is called an earthquake. An earthquake occurs when the tectonic plates move alongside each other. When plates moving in opposite directions lock on to each other, pressure begins to build before they jolt past each other. This jolt sends *SEISMIC WAVES* toward the surface, and these make the ground shake back and forth.

Earthquakes are one of the most damaging natural disasters created by our planet's four elements.

GOOD VIBRATIONS

The worst damage on land occurs directly above the place that the locked plates break. This is called the epicenter. The vibrations felt on the ground can be big enough to knock you off your feet or small enough that you don't even notice. Most of the earthquakes that take place every year can hardly be felt at all.

FAULT SCARP

FAULT

EPICENTER

FOCUS

WAVE FRONTS

When an earthquake's epicenter is in an ocean, the vibrations may cause a *TSUNAMI*. This is one way the elements work together.

The epicenter is the place on land directly above the focus, which is the place in the earth that the earthquake started.

RICHTER AND MERCALLI

The methods we use to measure the **MAGNITUDE** of an earthquake date back over a hundred years. In 1935, an American **SEISMOLOGIST** named Charles Richter put together a numbered scale that helped scientists measure the strength of earthquakes, which we call the Richter scale. At the turn of the 20th century, Italian **VOLCANOLOGIST** Giuseppe Mercalli had also put together a more descriptive scale, which was used to understand the destruction an earthquake might cause, but we don't use this scale as much today.

After the first wave of large vibrations ends, the earthquake isn't necessarily over—other smaller sets of vibrations can follow. These are called aftershocks.

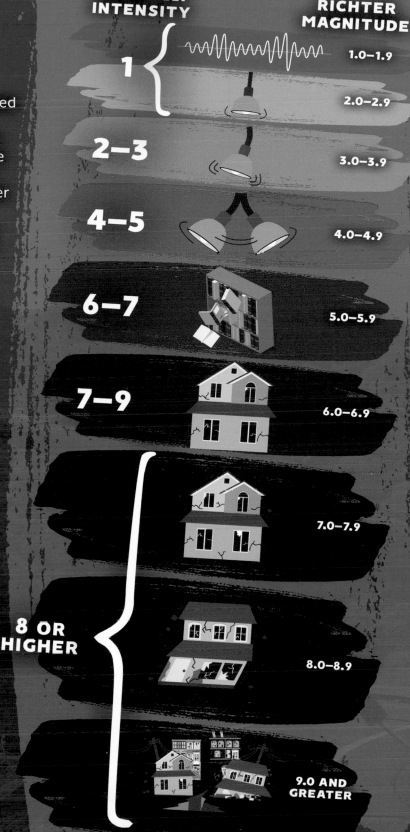

MERCALLI INTENSITY	RICHTER MAGNITUDE
1	1.0–1.9
	2.0–2.9
2–3	3.0–3.9
4–5	4.0–4.9
6–7	5.0–5.9
7–9	6.0–6.9
	7.0–7.9
8 OR HIGHER	8.0–8.9
	9.0 AND GREATER

WHEN IT ALL COMES TUMBLING DOWN

When an earthquake's magnitude measures very high on the Richter scale, it is very likely that huge amounts of damage will be caused. Earthquakes have been known to make buildings completely collapse, cause highways to crumble, and completely crack the ground in half. Earthquakes are usually responsible for lots of people losing their lives, too, making them one of the deadliest natural disasters.

AFTER THE AFTERSHOCKS

A HELPING HAND

When an area has been damaged badly by the effects of an earthquake, lots of **ORGANIZATIONS** and countries will usually send supplies such as water, food, and medical equipment to help the survivors of the natural disaster. The aim is to help survivors stay healthy and get the treatment they need, ready for the long and difficult task of rebuilding their communities.

These supplies are being prepared to help disaster victims.

THE BIG FIX

Organizations like Disaster Aid International and the Red Cross also send equipment to help communities rebuild their homes and **INFRASTRUCTURE**. By providing home repair kits and water filters, unaffected countries can work together and help to provide **AID** for those in need.

Some organizations send out lots of doctors, builders, and engineers to help the countries affected by disaster.

HAITI 2010 EARTHQUAKE

Many of the world's largest earthquakes have an epicenter away from land, out in the sea. In these cases, it is usually the resulting tsunami that causes the biggest amount of damage to nearby countries. However, in 2010, an earthquake with a magnitude of 7.0 on the Richter scale occurred directly beneath the Caribbean country of Haiti. The size of the earthquake brought Haiti to its knees, causing buildings to collapse and killing hundreds of thousands of people.

Haiti's capital city, Port–au–Prince, was badly damaged in the earthquake.

HELPING HAITI

Rescue efforts began as soon as the earthquake had finished, with aims of finding people trapped in the rubble of collapsed buildings and supplying medical aid to those who had been injured. In the weeks and months after, countries across the planet pledged *RESOURCES* and funding to Haiti, such as the United States, which donated $48 million to the relief efforts.

Over the first weekend following the disaster, Haiti received: 130,000 food packets, 70,000 water containers, 2,000 rescuers, 161 search dogs, and 559,000 pounds (250 metric tons) of supplies.

medical aid being prepared in Haiti

11

MOUNTAINS AND VOLCANOES

The element of earth does not just describe the flat ground we stand on or the tectonic plate jigsaw puzzle beneath it. It also includes the tallest points on our planet. The mountains that soar high up through the clouds also support life the same way that earth does lower down, but they can also be just as destructive.

MAKING MOUNTAINS

Most mountains are formed when Earth's tectonic plates push toward each other. The pressure, from millions of years of pushing, forces the tectonic plates to fold upward, creating huge protruding areas of land, which we call mountains. The tallest mountain in the world is found in the Himalayas in Asia. Its name is Mount Everest and it reaches over 29,000 feet (8,848 m) into the sky, making it the highest point on Earth.

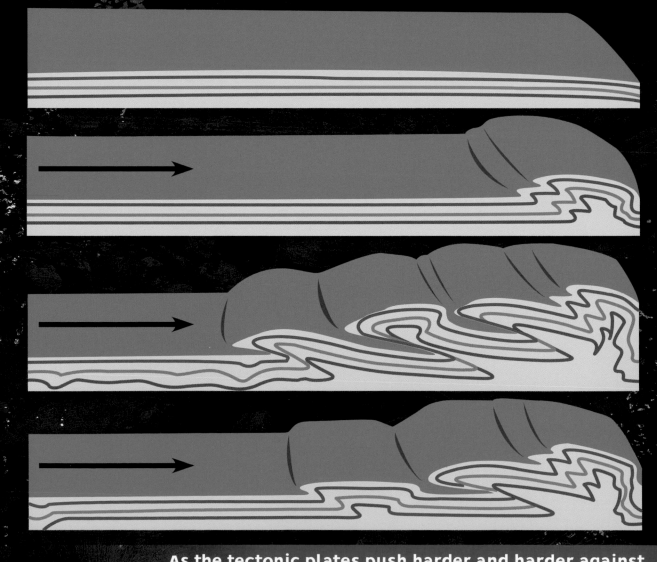

As the tectonic plates push harder and harder against each other, the mountain folds grow higher and higher.

RISING TEMPERATURES

Not all mountains are harmless areas of land; some have an opening at the top, called a vent, that funnels all the way down to the **MOLTEN ROCK** below the crust. These mountains are called volcanoes. The way that volcanoes are formed is slightly different than regular mountains. They are created when **MAGMA** from Earth's core pushes up through an opening in the tectonic plates and erupts. As the magma cools on the surface, it becomes hard rock and eventually begins to layer up, growing into a bigger mountain with each eruption.

SHAPES AND SIZES

Depending on the type of molten rock that erupts from a volcano's vent, a volcano might become any one of four different shapes and sizes.

STRATOVOLCANO

THESE ARE THE TALLEST TYPES OF VOLCANO AND THEY HAVE VERY STEEP SLOPES WITH MANY SECONDARY VENTS.

SHIELD

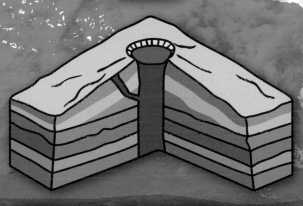

THESE ARE THE LARGEST TYPES OF VOLCANO. THEY HAVE LONG, GENTLE SLOPES.

CINDER CONE

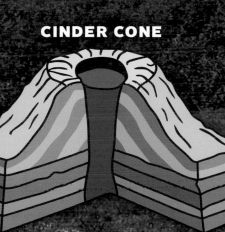

THESE VOLCANOES ARE TALL AND STEEP, BUT ONLY HAVE ONE MAIN VENT.

CALDERA

THESE ARE NAMED AFTER THEIR CAULDRON-LIKE SHAPE AND LARGE VENT.

DELVING DEEP

MAIN VENT

THIS IS WHERE THE MAJORITY OF THE MOLTEN ROCK ERUPTS FROM THE VOLCANO. IT IS THE LARGEST OPENING IN THE MOUNTAIN AND IS CONNECTED DIRECTLY TO THE MAGMA CHAMBER BELOW EARTH'S CRUST. MAGMA THAT HAS LEFT THE VOLCANO IS CALLED LAVA.

LAYERS

VOLCANOES GROW EVERY TIME THEY ERUPT. LAYERS OF LAVA AND ASH FROM EACH ERUPTION BUILD UP ON TOP OF EACH OTHER AND TURN SOLID, INCREASING THE SIZE OF THE VOLCANO.

SECONDARY VENT

SHIELD VOLCANOES AND STRATOVOLCANOES BOTH NORMALLY HAVE A SET OF SECONDARY VENTS. THESE ARE MUCH SMALLER OPENINGS IN THE SURFACE THAT ARE STILL CONNECTED TO THE MAIN CHAMBER, MEANING LAVA CAN ESCAPE HERE TOO.

MAGMA CHAMBER

MAGMA IS MOLTEN ROCK THAT SITS UNDERNEATH EARTH'S CRUST. IT RISES FROM EARTH'S MANTLE AND GATHERS IN A CHAMBER BELOW A VOLCANO. WHEN TOO MUCH MAGMA IS STORED IN THIS CHAMBER, PRESSURE BUILDS UP AND MAKES THE MAGMA SHOOT UP THROUGH THE VOLCANO'S VENT.

FAULTY CONNECTIONS

Where two tectonic plates meet and move toward, away from, or alongside each other, fault lines are normally created. Faults are sections of Earth's crust that have cracked and either slipped or separated, causing magma to rise up through the space and cool to form new rock. Fault lines are characterized by large cracks in the earth. These can be found on land or underwater in lots of places across the planet.

fault line in Peru

SAN ANDREAS

One of the most famous fault lines in the world is the San Andreas Fault in the United States. It runs through California for around 745 miles (1,200 km). When the fault moves, this is usually in a jolting motion for a distance of around 2 inches (5 cm). This might not sound like much, but this is enough to cause seismic waves big enough for an earthquake!

Californians live in fear of "the Big One"—an earthquake measuring very high on the Richter scale. Some people believe it is inevitable and that it will happen in the near future.

RING OF FIRE

Volcanoes always appear above faults in Earth's crust, because this is where the surface splits enough to let magma rise up and cool to form solid rock. In the Pacific Ocean, a 24,800-mile (40,000 km) horseshoe-shaped belt of fault lines is home to 452 volcanoes. It is known as the Ring of Fire. This belt is home to over 75% of our planet's active and **DORMANT VOLCANOES**!

An active volcano is one that has erupted at least once in the last 10,000 years.

INDIAN OCEAN TSUNAMI

The Ring of Fire is not just responsible for creating volcanoes. As some of the underwater fault lines slip, they create seismic waves big enough to disturb the ocean. When the seismic waves are big enough, they might trigger a tsunami, such as the Indian Ocean tsunami of 2004. The underwater earthquake reached a 9.0 magnitude on the Richter scale, spawning tsunami waves that reached heights of up to 98 feet (30 m). Nearly 230,000 people lost their lives in the tsunami, making it the deadliest natural disaster of the 21st century.

Lots of countries surrounding the Indian Ocean were affected by the tsunami, including India, Indonesia, Sri Lanka, and Thailand.

WASTING
THE EARTH

While earth can be one of the deadliest and most destructive elements, it can also be destroyed by humans. One of the most common ways humans have damaged the earth is by filling it with our waste. For years, we have removed large areas of soil and plants to fill the ground with our garbage. These areas are called landfill sites. Not only is landfill horrible to look at, it is also very dangerous for our planet.

Over 2,000 landfill sites are dotted around the United States today.

TOXIC TROUBLE

Large pits are dug and garbage is thrown in, then often covered over with the same soil removed from the pit. During periods of heavy rainfall, water can soak through this soil, trickle through the waste, and soak into the ground. During this process, lots of *TOXIC CHEMICALS* can gather in the water and transfer into the soil. Not only does this harm animals that live in the soil, but it also fills nearby rivers and lakes with toxic chemicals as the water travels through the ground.

The toxic chemicals carried by water into rivers and lakes can kill the fish that live in them.

IT'S A TRAP!

Lots of the waste that we put into landfill is made up of **ORGANIC** objects. These objects are biodegradable, which means they break down naturally over time. However, while this is better than materials that don't naturally **DECOMPOSE** going into landfill, such as plastic, these biodegradable organic objects release harmful gases into the atmosphere when they decompose. They release a gas called methane, which is a **GREENHOUSE GAS**. Greenhouse gases pollute the air and trap heat in Earth's atmosphere, which leads to global warming.

Global warming is the gradual increase in temperature on our planet. This is mostly a result of human activity, such as burning different fuels.

Food is a type of organic object that decomposes in landfill.

EVICTION NOTICE

For any animals that might be living on the land, being moved to create space for a landfill site has huge consequences. It has been estimated that the creation of landfill sites can amount to the loss of hundreds of species of animals.

While many animals may lose their home to landfill sites, other animals, such as gulls, flock to them to find food.

LIFE IN THE GROUND

When we aren't feeling the destructive force of Earth, or we aren't in the process of destroying it ourselves, earth is an element that can support and sustain life across the entire planet. Vibrant communities of animals and plants around the world use earth as their home and their source of food and water all year round.

HOME IS WHERE THE EARTH IS

There are millions of species of animals on our planet, many of which live underground. Insects, mammals, and even some birds are among many types of animals that make a home out of the earth beneath our feet. Many animals, such as ants, make entire nests underground, with tunnel connections between different sections, almost like a big city with lots of roads!

Every ant **COLONY** has a queen ant. She is usually the mother of every ant in the colony and can have thousands of ants working for her at one time!

Ants will leave the nest to collect food and other materials and then return to the colony many times in a single day.

GETTING TO THE ROOT OF THINGS

Plants depend on earth even more than many animals. Without it, most plants could not exist. Earth provides plants with a way to **ANCHOR** themselves to stay in place and stand upright, as well as providing them with the vital **NUTRIENTS** that they need to stay alive. Soil has lots of important nutrients in it that plants need to survive. These nutrients **DISSOLVE** in water, which plants **ABSORB** through their roots.

If you lined up all the roots of a fully grown grass plant, they could measure over 320 feet (100 m)!

STANDING STRONG

Roots are especially important during extreme weather conditions. Plants use a network of long roots that branch out underground to cover a large **SURFACE AREA**. The more spread out their roots are, the more the plant is anchored into the soil and is less likely to be pulled out of the ground. Without their roots, plants wouldn't be able to keep themselves in one place in order to absorb nutrients and grow.

Roots keep most plants in place during very strong winds and heavy rain.

BUILDING FROM THE GROUND UP

For thousands of years, humans have been using different types of earth to build with. From very old techniques such as wattle and daub, to modern techniques such as bricks and mortar, earth has always been used to build structures for humans to live in and take shelter from the outdoors.

Mud is still used to build houses and other buildings all over the world today.

IN A MUD-DLE

Using mud to build huts and houses is one of the oldest construction techniques on the planet. To build a mud wall, wet mud is taken from the ground and molded into the base of a wall by hand. Then, the base is left to dry out until it turns hard. The process is repeated over and over again until all of the walls are tall enough for people to stand up and live inside.

mud buildings, Morocco

WATTLE AND DAUB

For over 6,000 years, humans have been using a technique to build using earth, called wattle and daub. Wattle is a set of flexible wooden branches that have been woven together to form a type of fence-like structure. This section forms the base to build around. To pad out the wall, a combination of wet soil, clay, straw, and sometimes animal poop is pressed onto the wattle and left to dry. This sticky mixture is the daub.

Using wattle to build walls makes them much sturdier than just using mud. This helps when the other three natural elements are at their most fearsome.

This school in Kenya was built using wattle and daub.

YOU'RE FIRED!

The most common way we see earth used for building houses in today's modern cities and towns is brickwork. Bricks are usually made from clay, which is a natural combination of rock and soil *MINERALS*. Once clay has been shaped into a brick, it is put into a fired kiln, which is like a large oven for cooking bricks until they become hard. Fired clay bricks are one of the most sturdy materials for building walls.

POWER PLAYS

So we know earth is useful for building with, but earth can also help out around the house in ways you wouldn't expect. The electricity powering your television, the energy powering your school's lights, the charge used to power a smartphone—earth can be used to make all of these things. Obviously we don't plug our phones straight into the ground: that would be very silly! However, earth is used to generate electricity in lots of places across the world.

GOING GEOTHERMAL

The earth beneath our feet generates a lot of heat energy. The heat comes from the center of the planet and is contained in the rocks below Earth's surface. This heat can produce steam by heating water anywhere from a few feet below Earth's surface to several miles down. We can use this heat to produce the electricity that powers our cities and homes. We call this geothermal energy.

At the center of Earth, called the core, the temperature is thought to be around 10,800°F (6,000°C)!

The center of Earth is so hot that it can heat pools of water on its outer surface.

MAKING HEAT WITH HEAT

By funneling down into the earth beneath us, we can make use of the heat energy stored under the surface of our planet. We can use a geothermal heat pump to extract heat from the ground and use it to power the heating system in a house. We can also use a source of steam underground to drive a turbine above the ground, which powers a generator that supplies our homes and schools with electrical energy.

TURBINE   GENERATOR

STEAM

HOT WATER

GOT IT ON REPEAT

Geothermal energy is an example of a renewable energy source. A renewable energy source is something we can get energy from that will never run out. Renewable energy sources are good for the environment because they don't release any harmful chemicals into the atmosphere. Nonrenewable energy sources such as coal, oil, and gas, however, will run out. Burning these energy sources to make electricity releases huge amounts of carbon dioxide into our atmosphere, which increases the effect of global warming on our planet.

geothermal power plant, Iceland

Other examples of renewable energy sources are: water, wind, and the light from the sun.

CELEBRATING THE EARTH

Earth and soil can be very useful for human activity. Earth is also an element that is celebrated across the planet. A festival is an event where many people come together to celebrate a part of their **CULTURE**. There are many festivals across the world that either celebrate or include earth in some way.

MAKING A MESS

Every year, people around the world celebrate their love for the earth beneath them. None, however, celebrate it quite like South Korea. Every summer they host a mud festival. Here, people can slide through, dive into, and wrestle in wet and gloopy mud, all while listening to Korean musicians and singers perform live on stage!

The South Korean Mud Festival was created to bring attention to the mud flats in Boryeong, which are said to contain minerals that are good for the skin.

FOOD, GLORIOUS FOOD

One of the most common celebrations of the soil and its ability to create and sustain plant life are the yearly harvest festivals around the world. The harvest season is the time of year in each country that crops are ready to be gathered from the ground and used for food. Yearly harvest festivals are an ancient celebration of crops produced in soil that still takes place today, where farmers bring a selection of their fruit and crops to be enjoyed and celebrated by everyone.

Harvest festivals around the world are often religious festivals.

Harvest season is different for countries across the planet. This is because the four seasons happen at different times of the year depending on where you are in the world.

AT ONE WITH NATURE

People believe in the power of the earth so much that we even make cosmetics using mud! Cosmetics are products we can buy at stores that improve the way we look. Some people buy mud masks, which they apply to the skin on their face or body and leave until it's dry. When it's dry, they wash it off to reveal healthy, clean, smooth skin!

WORSHIPPING THE GROUND WE WALK ON

We normally understand the four elements in terms of the science behind them. We know how they occur, how they work, and how we can use them. However, for lots of people around the world, religion can apply other meanings to the elements. The gods of many religions are believed to control the elements. Earth is usually thought to be used for creation by different gods.

REIGN OF TERRA

The people of ancient Rome believed Earth was ruled over by different gods. Terra was believed to be one of the most powerful goddesses of all—she was Mother Nature. She was believed to be responsible for the creation of life and productivity of the earth. She was honored at ancient Roman festivals that celebrated the *FERTILITY* of the land and good crops.

Terra's full name was Terra Mater, which translates into English as Mother Earth.

Roman depiction of Mother Earth

GIFT OF THE GEB

Just like the ancient Romans, the ancient Egyptians worshipped many gods. They were believed to oversee different parts of the universe. The ancient Egyptian god of earth was called Geb. It was believed that he allowed crops to grow from the land, that he placed minerals and precious rocks in the ground, and that when he laughed, his laughter created earthquakes!

The ancient Egyptians called Geb *Kenkenwer*, which means "the Great Cackler."

WE ALL HAVE TO MAKE SACRIFICES

Many people who lived near volcanoes used to associate them with something religious or **MYTHOLOGICAL**. It's easy to see why, as they can give life to thousands of crops with their fertile land or they can take life away with their deadly eruptions. Some people used to believe that they could get their gods to have mercy on them by completing **RITUALS**. One of the most common ancient rituals was to sacrifice an animal by throwing it into the volcano to stop the gods from making it erupt!

People leave all kinds of offerings to volcanoes, including food, plants, and even animals!

IN CASE OF EMERGENCY

It's unlikely you'll ever be in a very powerful earthquake, but if you ever are, there are five important things you should do to stay safe.

1 PREPARE!
If you live in a country that is at risk of an earthquake, make sure you have a plan for where you would go and take cover.

2 DROP AND COVER!
As soon as you feel a significant rumble, drop to the floor and take cover under a desk or a table.

3 FURNITURE!
Stay away from any tall or wobbly pieces of furniture that could fall on you, such as a bookcase.

4 WINDOWS!
Stay away from windows as they may break during the earthquake.

5 AFTERSHOCKS!
After the shaking has finished, remember to expect aftershocks—the earthquake might not be over yet!

GLOSSARY

ABSORB	to take in or soak up
AID	support given by governments or charities in a time of disaster, such as food or money
ANCHOR	to hold something firmly in place
CARBON DIOXIDE	a natural, colorless gas that is found in the air
CIVILIZATIONS	the societies, cultures, and ways of life of certain areas
COLONY	a group of plants or animals living or growing in one place
CONTINENTS	very large areas of land that are made up of many countries, such as Africa and Europe
CRUST	the hard, outermost layer of Earth
CULTURE	the traditions, ideas, and ways of life of a particular group of people
DECOMPOSE	to decay and rot
DISSOLVE	to become part of a liquid
DORMANT VOLCANOES	volcanoes that are not currently active, but could become active at any time
FAULTS	breaks in Earth's crust
FERTILITY	the ability to support the growth and life of a plant
GREENHOUSE GAS	a gas in the atmosphere that traps the sun's heat
INFRASTRUCTURE	the equipment and structures that a country needs to function properly, such as roads and bridges
MAGMA	hot liquid rock below the surface of Earth
MAGNITUDE	the power of an earthquake
MANTLE	a layer of Earth made up of semi-molten rock
MATTER	substances from which things are made
MINERALS	important things that plants, animals, or humans need to grow
MOLTEN ROCK	rock that is so hot that it has turned to a liquid substance, usually found in Earth's mantle
MYTHOLOGICAL	relating to, based on, or appearing in myths
NUTRIENTS	natural substances that are needed for plants to grow
ORGANIC	made of living matter
ORGANIZATIONS	companies, businesses, or charities formed for a particular purpose
OXYGEN	a natural gas that all living things need in order to survive
PHILOSOPHY	the study of the nature of knowledge, reality, and existence
PHOTOSYNTHESIZE	the process by which plants turn energy from sunlight into food
PLASMA	gases in which a large amount of the molecules are ionized
RESOURCES	supplies of money, materials, or people
RITUALS	ordered actions that take place during religious ceremonies
SEISMIC WAVES	vibrations that travel through Earth
SEISMOLOGIST	a person who studies earthquakes
SURFACE AREA	the amount of space covered by the surface of something
TOXIC CHEMICALS	substances that are harmful to the environment
TSUNAMI	a very large wave caused by an earthquake
VOLCANOLOGIST	a person who studies volcanoes
VOLUME	the amount of space that a 3-D object takes up

INDEX